ACCORDING TO LILIES

According to Lilies

ROGER FINCH

CARCANET

First published in 1992 by
Carcanet Press Limited
208-212 Corn Exchange Buildings
Manchester M4 3BQ

A CIP catalogue record of this book is
available from the British Library.
ISBN 0 85635 932 7

The publisher acknowledges financial assistance
from the Arts Council of Great Britain

Set in 10pt Palatino by Bryan Williamson, Darwen
Printed and bound in England by SRP Ltd, Exeter

In memory
of my mother
Phyllis Ivy Finch

Contents

The 3.05 Train Passes in the Night, Three Minutes Late

He is not asleep. Each night at three o'clock
his doll's eyes click open, staring straight above
at the ceiling rocked by the country streetlight
rocked by the wind. He's waiting for the long wail
of the 3.05 train to whoop nearly upright

in his room above the whirlpooling wheels,
waiting for its long wire of ooooo's to pull taut
and snap at last on the horizon. His eyes
are open. If I look close, I'll see them glint
with the same moonlight that just at noon will rise

and rub against the peachbloom-glaze-coloured skin
of China's velvet peaches. He could be boy
or girl. The dark's indiscriminate fingers
nightmoth above the androgynous fear-lit lantern
of his beauty. The fire of others' faces lingers

beneath the paper nautilus shell of his face;
infects the waxwork hands lying lily-limp
on top of the Flying Geese design of the quilt.
The train is three minutes late. It's three minutes late
because it takes three minutes to note the tilt

of lamplight through the window, the gesso mask
against the plaster pillow with moonlight's gilt
drizzling from small square books on its underground.
Even now he is waiting for me to write
the train into this poem, waiting for the sound

of it to crumple the right side of the page
and to tear out through the left, waiting for me
to finish writing and put aside my pen,
waiting for his soul with the thunder of trains
to fall from me back into childhood's body again.

Ring Taw

Early spring, and the world is puddle-sweet.
　　We boys gang in Ricky's yard
and there, down there on the hard-packed clay,
where no grass and scarcely any weed will grow,
　　we scuff, by shoetip or stick,
the magic circle. This showcase is too rough
　　for the treasure that we will strew there:
aggies and steelies, rainbows, milkies, cat's-eyes
　　and clearies. The random colours riff

　　as the cloud cover tears and the sun
　　　runs through and scrabbles them. Chilblains
(we have often been warned of this) clang
through our legs as we kneel on the clammy earth.
　　The shooter's knees, rouged with mud,
are now at nose height as he stands; they give off
　　the fragrance of rust or rotten fruit.
One by one we knuckled down. The bright eye flares
　　as it knocks *click! click!* against the scruff

　　of a fine fat shiner, spins it out
　　　and burns on back. One by one
　　the swirled, scaled, scrolled, mottled, peacock-tailed,
and mushroom-gilled glassies vanish into the swag
　　of the stronger ones. Fewer
and fewer can play. Vanquished in the first trials,
　　I hang back and watch my baubles pass
hand to hand. In the twilight they glint, not beads now
　　but bloodstones and tourmalines, real jewels.

'September Morn'

To the boy in the barber chair
in his grandfather's basement,
the 1920's Harlowe-blonde nude
posed on a rock in a pool
in front of a calendar-blue sky,
one arm stretched coyly forward as though to lift
the swallowtail perched on it,
is a fairy. Where are the wings? The heading says
'September Morn'. Her right leg bends to her left

to hide the red-gold delta.
Men, he-men, want to see that.
The boy (is he ten? eleven? twelve?)
is still free of centrefold
interests. His gaze slides like a cat's
toward anything colourful: syrups on the shelf,
the reds and ambers and greens
(a street-light blend) of Wildroot and Lucky Tiger.
His ears lap up his grandfather's gentle laugh;

he nuzzles the aromas
of witch hazel and bay rum
over fresh laundry and Bulldog bleach,
home-made elderberry wine.
We want to hold the hours we squirmed through,
not in the mind but in the hand, feel the gnarls
worn smooth, unreasonable
demand, but human. We want to see the light
glint dully on the fresh-shorn, dark, once-golden curls.

Peacock on Top of the House

Detail of an illustration from the manuscript
of Amaru Sataka. Rajasthani School. Circa 1680 AD

The illustration is entitled
'Heroine Waiting for Her Lover'. She sits
    inside, against a cinnabar-red

background, imperturbably smoking
a nargileh or 'water pipe'. She's clearly not
    the heroine of *Erwartung* with her fits

of near-hysteria, fingernails pressed
painfully into palms, and the half chant/half screams
    that pose as song. She's immersed in thought,

and her mind is ingrained 'forebearing'.
We know this from the colour of the sari she wears:
    indigo sprinkled with small moonbeams

of sequin silver disposed in four-leaf
clovers, and from the peacock perched on the roof,
    denoting 'tranquillity' (though his airs

are hardly tranquil, seem rather to our ears
to spell 'alarm!'). This label may have been won
    from the way he holds himself aloof,

the way he trails by, ponderously,
languorously, betraying his near-serpent
    ancestry as he goose-necks from one

side to the other. His cry is the first
note, *sa*, of the seven-note Indian scale.
    They must feel that artistry is meant

by that, when in fact it is more strident
than Schoenberg's soprano. And yet we admire
    the brooch of his form with its furled tail

inlaid in the indigo platter
of the sky, as champlevé enamels are laid,
    their frits and glass pastes fused in the fire

and then smoothed and polished. He stands out
conspicuously against his mounting, unlike
    'Peacock in the Woods' (a study made

by Abbott Thayer for 'Concealing-
Coloration in the Animal Kingdom'),
    though 'mounting' here is not designed to strike

the eye necessarily as jewellery.
Few jewels can imitate him: amethyst,
    emerald, topaz; they capture the sum

of his colours but they cannot catch
his iridescent feathers. We need the bee's-wing
    mica magic of the ceramist

for this, his lustreware glazes of spun
goldgreen copper and smoky plum-purple that match
    the peacock as he opens in the sun.

What Is Written in Rooms

Time. Decay. Run your fingers across
the top of the Hepplewhite sideboard.
The roan-red mahogany heartwood
will bleed through. The gloss on horses' flanks
still pulses beneath the velvet dust
that has volcanic ash from craters
in Mexico in it, the papery mud

from wasps' nests, mica flakes from gnats' wings,
pollen grains that lavender foxtail grass
in the fall, fine flour of plaster that sifts
piecemeal from the ceiling. Try to recall
this room when alive. Wax made agate,
tiger's-eye and jasper of woodwork;
spidery lace and lacy papercrafts

made baby's-breath around the windows;
Belfast glass prisms flashed dragonfly
rainbows across the lilypond walls.
When Grandmother died, three daughters took down
the sea-at-night-blue silks; their arms sank
in heavy waves edged with whitecap fringe
as they laid them out in long canals

to wind them up. After a few years,
closed rooms begin to wear the sheer veils
women in the 1930s wore
over their faces. You think you see
a shrouded nun, though, stifle the sun
as the clock's throat hangs at an ancient six
and spring-turned stars step back where they were.

Sunday Painter

The distant hills are a glaze of lavender
    over Veronese green, like sprigs
of asparagus nudging their pearly sheen
through a crust of earth. The blue satin sky rigs

its clouds in a most intriguing way, trying
    out tottering towers and swans' wings
in a fit of heavenly jugglery. The lake
below has a taste for the sky's pretty things,

wearing its wide mantle like the Virgin's robe;
    no slab of lapis lazuli could
be more bluely blue, blueing the sky's laundry
before it throws it back, touching up the woods

that stretch across it toward the gathering eye.
    My mother paints a scene. Shut away
high in an upstairs room, where the gaze can lean
like a balcony over the bolt of day

unrolled for its inspection, she is seated
    within a cloud of spirited scent
that haunts the room: the lilac of terpineol;
pungent oil of spike. But what she paints is pent

up on the wall in front of her: a landscape
    by Corot with its egg-whisk trees that part
the sky and froth the light; and her brush acquires
it by second nature through the eye of art.

What Is Written on the Floor

A trapdoor of light:
a Naples-yellow rhomboid
with a bar (curiously) across its centre
like the one across the centre of the window.
            No, a pool.
On its skin float loops of indigo

            and ultramarine
        and manganese violet
and alizarin crimson that are slobber
from my palette. The colours skein and marble,
            constructing
little eddies and maelstroms and artful

        cascades that are apt
    to impart their taffeta
designs to the endpapers laid on their surface.
I sit at the edge of the pool and dabble
            my legs down.
Honey-warm! Honey from the chapel

        of its broken comb
    flowing out in fused amber
confusion, the flecks of bee's-wax trapped in it
thinned by the sun and mixed with it. Bronze shadows
            start and dart
from under the rafters. They are minnows

        or Eocene flies.
    Beneath them the weightier
and more gradual golds, goldsilvers and pewter
grays of carps' bodies glide beyond the molten
            underfoot
    ceilings that are their skies. A golden

Aladdin's door-ring
magically appears. I pull,
and suddenly I cascade down a sepia
Tiepolo heaven showering swarms of *putti*
as ochre
and umber and orotund as woolly

bumblebees. Are the fish
cupids or the cupids fish?
Certainly the dome is Heaven, for a real
Assumption is stuck inside it. It is odd,
however,
that no one notices the feet of God.

The Rape of Ganymede

By eagle's eye, the pubescence on the boy
    is visible as short gold wires. Zeus behind the eye
      sees millions of cells, each cell
    containing a yolk of energy.
    Just as the aggie is about to shoot
from the forefinger fold in front of the boy's thumb,
scattering reds, blues, and greens out of the ring,
    the gate of Heaven rattles its gongs
and Zeus descends the sky on a staircase of wings.

The boy is startled. His playmate, a cousin, runs.
    Later, the cousin will tell that the sea
      fell from the sky, the black waves on fire
    from core to snow-cap, the hammering
    against the air like the hammering of hands
against the heart. He does not understand love,
does not know why his friend did not thrust the flood
    away but stood dancing in it, a god
taking place in him as the sky danced in his blood.

His words will serve as sketch for workers in stone.
    One will show a teen-age boy at play
      with an eagle, one will show the bird
    lifting the boy, lifting its quarry.
    Stone cannot hold such motion. Only sound,
the rumblings in the lower strings, the troughs and crests
in the clarinets, the flutes high, high overhead,
    can portray the pair whirling out loud
as they bypass the cousin, arms and wings spread.

A Rare and Precious Fabric Woven of Friends

Veronica's veil is hardly more wondrous
    than this; nor is the Shroud of Turin
    with its particularly faithful
rendering of the Incarnate Face. Held up thus

against the light it is nothing singular;
    simply an old pongee handkerchief,
    notable more perhaps for its hue
than for anything else: rather similar

to peach-skin with its velvety digressions
    from deep rose to the very palest
    orange. But, steeped within the sun's quick
mordant, moiré forms appear, like impressions

jotted down on two curtains that are shedded,
    one above, one below the other,
    by the fingers of a summer breeze,
weaving the faces of friends. Some are threaded

firmly in the weft; others almost erased
    by time's astringent bleach: they shunt in
    and out, swiped by the shuttle's eye,
swiftly across the cloth, registered in haste,

puzzling as an indecipherable name.
    And then there are those so fugitive
    that they regret to appear unless
the cloth is candled by the tenderest flame.

Music Alcove, Northside Public Library

Three things marked that mezzanine:
the light, the heat, the dust. From the south,
radiance always poured. Oakwood glowed
in it. On those coals, Debussy's dreams
exhaled their frankincense. Flute, then harp,
then viola flowed across the page.
My hands reeked of musk where paper had touched them.
I read scores as most boys read mysteries;
as I read I waved a ghost wand and hummed out loud.

I imagined I was conducting
opera. Up on stage, the tenor longed
to send kisses up the long blonde bands
that streamed from the soprano's tower. I stood there
in the brambles with him, my mouth snagged
on fineness. I was also the cat face
that his kisses leapt for, silver'd by the moon.
A programme exists only if it has
an audience. I had mine, three vagabonds

who came to the library
to sleep through winter, still as Maeterlinck's
unnamed cripples. They gave off the throngs,
just as doubles emanate from Buddhist gods.
If the person in the tier above
had looked down, he would have seen my arms
slicing the gold-leafed morocco-bordered air
into onlookers, players, and parts
for motionless old men, my trio of strings.

The Wisteria that Strangled the House

For years it had been moving in for the kill.
   No one who saw its weight-lifter's trunk,
its superbly muscled limbs, would have denied
that it could do it. In the winter, the house
was an old bloodstone ball set in a puzzle
   of tarnished silver. In the summer,
   no one could recall that cankerous

colour beneath the green. In the spring, a small
   mauve mountain or tumulus surged up
where the house used to stand; for miles and miles around,
strangers wondered what noble Korean kings
were buried beneath its droning surfaces.
   During the height of the mating season
   the true dwellers slept as though dead, their tongues

coated with the male flowers' narcotic flavour.
   One night, as the dreamers drifted out
too far from shore, the vine tensed and clenched its hold
on the walls. It looked as though the house had donned
Medusa's hair as the vine squeezed hard. The house dropped
   its bird's bones through the victorious branches.
   The dreamers floated on in place, spellbound.

An Unknown Violinist Plays Harold in Italy

By the time he reached the third movement,
    the viola's soft arpeggio chords
processing in banners from the clerestory
    down the *Pilgrim's Hymn*'s tall muted nave,
Paganini was turned to tears. The panache
he would have paid for – devils' trills, hummingbirds
bursting into foxfire as they cleared the yards –

    had no place in this sequestered See
    of the spirit. Music of the ear,
on paper there was no flash, no fanfare, no *élan*.
    Now he would play it. And he would pay,
pay as Sultan Mahmūd of Ghazna vowed
to pay Firdausī, one couplet, one gold dinar,
for the *Shāh Nāmah*. He would not in the last hour

    renege, as the Sultan had reneged,
    awarding a paltry allowance,
the whole of which Firdausī gave 'to the bath-man
    and a sherbet-seller' as he left
the bath. The artist is easily open to wrath,
orders 'to be trampled to death by elephants'.
Paganini was a prince. There was high finance

    around his life. The tardy largesse,
    like the 60,000 dinars' worth
of indigo the Sultan finally sent,
    the camels bearing the gift through the East gate
just as Firdausī's corpse was borne out the West,
would enable Berlioz to live in wealth.
There was talk of live burial at Paganini's death.

Apsara

(Fundukistan, 7th Century)

Flower or flesh? This figure is both.
The hand with its orchidaceous petals swoons,
or else the petals are roots, they are being coaxed
    by moisture or earthiness to sprout.
    It may be from the body itself,
succulent, overripe, that this impulse swells,
like the aura of acetone from speckled fruit,

    a sympathetic magic that works
eye after eye of ornament from the skin,
a delicate tiara of leaves and hair
    offshooting from the topknot eyes, blanched
    to the whiteness of handkerchiefs
in the anterooms of temples. Serpent or man?
The hand's five tongues would flicker off if not cinched

    at the wrist by two bracelets; the arms
would worm into their earthly sheaths if not fused
to the torso, far too ponderous to drag.
    There are other ambiguities:
    the *apsaras* are heavenly nymphs,
'daughters of pleasure', the mistresses or wives
of the Gandharvas; this figure wins by ruse,

    for, though voluptuous, fair, unchaste,
he clearly is masculine: his bust is male,
his belly as adipose as a well-fed youth's.
    The viewer puts forth crown after crown
    of hunger: the hunger of the knife
for meat, the hunger of the worshipper's mouth
for prayers, tastes at once lewd, devout, urbane.

Cows in Moonlight

At first, it might have been the shadow of clouds
or trees on moon-frosted fields, but then you swerved
and your headlights picked out the couple-coloured beasts
pushing against the barbed wire, their leafy ears,
their gauzy new-mown-grass-scented breath twisted
toward you. Later you said a secret surprise
had you that night, you felt the tongues of your wrists

panting against the wheel, and wanted to stop.
You did not stop. You did not notice me crouched
naked in the overgrown nape of the field,
you did not see me stand, my long, cold flanks pressed
close to the rib cage of one cow as you passed,
trembling, you did not see that pair of mild eyes
wash me, as a lover's eyes would, as I held

her bristly hide against my belly. You caved
down the hill toward us and we clearly saw your face
backlit by your own headlights or by the thick
moonlight reaching in to you making a skull
of your wide black gaze. You did not hear our hooves
suck at the fruit-soft mud beneath spring sod
as we watched you, patient, wondering, not moonstruck.

On Stars: the Sempiternal Consciousness

We kept arguing about the stars.
There were only two of us but three voices.
You said the stars were luminous pips
in the universal fruit,
that watermelon ripening on Allah's vine.
The cosmos, like the melon,
must be an ellipse,

but I see stars as the atom's bees
glassily circling an invisible hive.
Otherwise they're phosphorescent curds
inside the cells in the mind
of God. All at once the genius among us
or madman (or both) piped up,
insisting the words

'God is within us' means precisely
that: the pith inside our receptacle flesh,
and that He exists in singular
splendour and is standing there
staring up at the seeds in our strawberry
hearts, wondering whatever
universe we are.

Learning to Apply Gilt

Journeyman, but not yet master,
I watch the master comb the gilder's brush
deftly through the short hairs on the side of his head
to charge it with static electricity
    and, touching it weightlessly to the brim
    of the goldleaf, draw the shimmering square
    from its book of jeweller's-rouged parchments
    across the oily membrane of the air
toward the waiting mordant to which it will adhere.

The room must be breathless. The gilder,
    too, must be breathless for the few moments
the goldleaf hangs from the lashes of his brush,
precariously full of life. It is tissue-thin,
    so sheer the window's letters are seen
    in reverse in the shadows of trees
    through its metal skin. In that instant
    it may tear, setting sparks off everywhere
like those goldfinch's feathers that fleck the atmosphere

of temples in Thailand. At times,
    the endlessness of the gold sheets may crack
as I fix them in place, letting through lightnings.
These may be revised, transplanting onto glass
    small costly flakes that float on the paths
    of my expiration. From afar,
    or at night, the effect is unbroken,
    but in noon's even light the mends may be found
in it which show mine was not the master's hand.

An Unrelenting Basso Ostinato

Toward the end of his mind, Schumann heard that one,
high, indelible note, E-flat, everywhere
wiring the air about him. It owed nothing
to nature. '*Zidaken*,' someone might have said
at first, 'Cicadas', when it was still a slight
but insinuating buzz snailed up inside
his cochlea. The truth is, the townspeople
heard nothing, they did not hear the trail of long
scarves behind his head as he passed, they noticed
only the staring gunshot wounds of the eyes
and the sharp cymbal crash as they fired. Other
sounds could not erase it. Birds were up against
it, leaving only barely discernible
prints of wings on its glassy persistence. Frogs,
crickets, bells, the wauling of cats, whatever
Düsseldorf had to offer, they were nothing,
less than nothing, less than the rustle of scores
beneath that overwhelming, agreed-on note
as the orchestra tunes up. Even his hands
could not march his piano's contrary chords
over it, could not cover it, no matter
how hard he played, no music could drown it out.

Such madnesses are rare. Imagine, if you will,
a ringing in the air that is always with you,
always E-flat, from the first notion of morning
up to the drop-in-bed-exhausted failure
to sleep because of it at night. At first he wove
a whole symphony around it, finally
admitting it was there, but how many works
could he write totally committed to one key?

Perhaps his ears put up for years with a chirp
in the floor or a squeaking gate that conferred
on him the above E-flat. We can achieve
a very artful effect by laying the best
Turkish paper on colours floating in a tray
of size. This owes nothing to nature. It may,

however, duplicate the gauze of fancy
in complexity and richness of colours,
may even duplicate the marblings of the mind
as it moves from one stunning enharmonic
progression to another. True genius speaks,
though, only as it tries to whip itself from the lime
of the branch, the throbbing of wings, the dissenting
minor ninth above the dominant chord of death.

How Certain Revolving Motions Become
Frozen in Time

Think how the circling, circling of rats
must stop as my fingers' forceps close around
their naked pink tails. Time, gauged by the stubborn
rotating wires we call 'hands', so runs down on the wrist
    of someone who cannot wear a watch.
'You'll have to throw them down much harder than that.'
    The last one did not die; his legs twitch

    with their delicate leaf-bud feet curled
in imagined pleading. Think of the ivory
toothpick teeth, the pink spinel eyes, the escapement
heart still ticking inside its ivory case
    of bones under the skin. If I press

    the mussed belly fur, it becomes plush,
as soft as ermine; I can feel the injured
fifing breath stutter in and out beneath it.
If I train my eye on the maddening pinwheel
    whirl of the drum in their cage, my mind
may whip up into spittlebug froth around
    its anger. Think of the jewellery bones, cleaned

    of flesh, more involved than a love-knot,
more intricate than an orrery of brass
with beads of agate, onyx, jasper and glass
for sun and planets, that is perfectly aligned
    but motionless, and must be moved by hand.

The Night After Beethoven's Last Piano Sonata

Adagio molto semplice e cantabile

       Your body is so like mine
   that if we changed brain and blood and bone
         I would lie perfectly
in you. It is wrong to want you. As I rust
   in bed, face up, the last luminous chords
   catch my skin; the impossible trills
tremble along by nerve point, a horse's itch.
      The night clouds me with its fragrance.
By the time you come I will be so dark that your touch

      will never reach me. The sky
   sheds its stars and still you do not come.
       You sit in mezzotint
replaying your sudden *sforzando*, a dance
   into heat-lightning, and your heart pales.
   It is terrible to want you. When we change
brain and blood and bone I will lie in my difference
     next, no, nearest to you. Your soul
is so like mine that I savour the distance.

Cherry Blossom Viewing

At the end of March each year,
  or April's first, a flowery madness
lies down all over Japan, sprawling from the south.
Their poets have compared it to moth-made clouds,
      but it is not moth,
  it's cotton candy cloying the trees,
  overly feminine and slightly
  distasteful. We shun parks and their crowds,

  the old ones keylessly singing,
    drive hours to observe the pale pink lace
of our own one tree against bottle-green pines,
the blue-and-white-striped sky our only curtain.
      How saké refines
  our passion! We do not seem to feel
  the roughed-by-winter wind on our skin
  as we cast off clothes in uncertain

    seclusion, so beautiful
  is the bloom of me against your bloom,
the scattered blossoming of my branches beyond
your body's threshold. The cherry trees unfold
      and small pink fragments
  speckle the glassy and ruddy gold
  of your naked shoulder. I watch you
  and faintly tremble, but not with cold.

What Is Written in Furniture

It doesn't tell you at first
how it owns you. You return one day to wade
through its shining satinwood waters.
You are fighting back its walnut waves;
your arms swim through its mahogany
sideboards, you are drowning in its Dutch armoires.
In Nishimura's prints, we see booksellers

with entire libraries wired
to their backs. Even today, vendors wander
Yuzawa's upland swamps, their bodies
exactly one-third of their wares. Thoreau
said, 'Simplify, simplify.' How can I
renounce the set of ten black lacquerware trays
with their leafgold and powdergilt birds, each species

a work of art, each unique?
An emperor might eat from them. Nightly fire
reaches for their incendiary
surfaces. I hear their tenants scream
through the braided bronze cage of my dreams.
As I bend with age, I shall bow with beauty,
a refuge for wings, an itinerant aviary.

A Fish Print

     The fisherman hauled
up the thing called 'saurel' or 'horse mackerel'
     like a fallen meteor
     heated to an incandescent green.
     It lay in the bottom of the boat
still fizzing and giving off sparks, its mouth filled
with murder and those delicate jeweller's teeth
as precise as a Sioux sunburst design quilled

     on buffalo hide,
its tail softly spanking the planks of the boat.
     Already its eye peered up
     through the milky cataract of death,
     fixed forever on some microscopic
fanfare in the sky. It was a record catch,
fit for pharaoh's pomp, gutted and spiced and glazed
with myrrh and fine damar to make its pelt match

     Mogul mail armour
with its overlapping scalloped copper scales,
     but you said the fisherman
     would take a print from it, braying it
     with charcoal ink, pressing its still-warm
coldblooded body on a sheet of hand-made
paper. And so he did, for when we went in
to dinner, there lay the fish with a cockade

     of paradisal
lemon, grilled a shade smaller than its shadow
     self now hanging on the wall
     behind it. I would impress my great
     inky self that way on your unprimed
memory, before your love eats me: wear it backed
by your own body, a ward against the chill
of forgetfulness, a closeness, a contact.

One of Japan's Earliest Musical Instruments, the Biwa

– to Teruo

In the illustrated scroll
of *The Tale of Genji*, we see the man bent
over the biwa's figgy form with its two
    crescent eyes bobbing up back-to-back
in a pulpy sky, mirroring precisely
the arch of the man's brows, but more seductive.
    The woman's face crouches in a crack

    of her kimono, so sleek
and so fat, a soybean popping from its husk,
beanlike in expression, beanlike in beauty.
    Persian poets invariably fit
the lover's face with a moon, but here I will
praise the man's face for its mooniness, stuck fast
    to the pasty shoulder like one bit

    of rice cake mounted upon
another. Here in the twentieth century
we have learned to smile at the biwa's buzzing,
    rather lemony notes, and as slips
glide like fingerlings through your grasp, I observe
how, even though the biwa's sound-holes were meant
    to copy human brows, yours eclipse

    the biwa's eyes in the way
they magnify your laughter. You do not fret
when your touch loses its foothold on a fret, but
    something mimic and wry monkeyshines
your face, gladdening me that the waxed and wooden
ways of love are of the past. Your fingers plunk!
    and plunk! just so, on the silky twines

        in the same way that you pluck
my chords. Then, when the song is done and we lose
our words, we slither into the brocade pod
        of sleep overembroidered with our charms
(though neither of us is moonlike or beanlike).
But I wake, and want you again, and slide down
        into the harmony of your arms.

Pavarotti Recalls Caruso,
But Who Will Recall Pavarotti?

His voice flows out of its golden comb
with not quite the nap of velvet and not quite
    the shimmer of silk.
There are infinitesimally small burrs
in it, just as Mélisande's ash-blonde tower
    shows by its roots, under microscope,
    its animal origin. We think
    sleek, black cat as Pavarotti purrs

'Una furtiva lagrima.' Mead
melts from aromatic jet in the retort
    of his throat. He sings
mezza voce, and the Great Caruso's voice
sifts into millions of shivering sunlight motes
    through the fine denier of time. There's moss
    in it; something erased; stiff as stone,
    and yet its gloss makes the touch rejoice,

like fingers that rub a stocking'd leg
catching on the nylon. The same voice will be
    all the more Caruso's
to a future race; or else their hands will tear
the disks out of their crusted Shang-bronze casings,
    and they will sail them, delightedly
    sail them, and Pavarotti's voice again
    will skip across and dazzle in the air.

On Looking into Chinggaltai's Grammar
of the Mongol Language

First there is the script:
gnarls of ancient wisteria;
   better yet, blackberry canes
that hold their icy early-morning fruit
just above the dust of goldenrod.
As I lift the book as though to drink
sweet white mare's milk from it, I smell the hair-long
   lemon-scented grasses of the steppe
   bruised by the hooves of Temujin's eight

   isabella geldings.
Then I see, written in eyelets and curls,
   the pronouns I have looked for:
the inclusive 'we' *bida*, the exclusive
'we' *ba*. The first one is 'you and I'
sharing on this page a membrane-thin
cross-section of my heart, under microscope
   a pomegranate freshly broken
   spitting its scores of garnets from the cove

   of a wine-washed rind.
The second is 'I and someone else'
   who lay together that day,
our skins shaded by the blackberry's leaves
shaded by honey locusts, our mouths
black-purple with its fruit's nearblack juice,
as though stained with the ink of fresh new pronouns
   as we took from each other a darker
   sweetness. Yet a third pronoun behaves

as both masculine
and feminine, pronoun for angels,
    who, we are told, are neither male
nor female. I would use it. I would speak
of the blackberry stain that stabbed through
your man's white shirt, making its birthmark
beneath, speak of how I lapped it from your flesh,
how goldenrod dusted your hair, how we cried
the same cry that angels make.

Incertezza del Poeta

– Giorgio de Chirico (1888-1978)

It is not
    merely not knowing which to portray,
      a headless female torso
or a bunch of bananas, each velvety spot
    on their leopard-yellow skin miming
      some small fleck of corruption
beneath her pearly husk; the poet must say

who he is
    today, old or young, woman or man,
      wise or feeble-minded. Words
require a transformation. Mirrors are his,
    holding in their icy walls a face
      that did not exist before;
he must mask his own with their quicksilver plan,

moulding clay,
    if he can, from his features – lines, planes,
      softened-by-sorrow contours.
The hunter learns to fear as he walks the way
    of tigers, sniffing in the fragrant spoor.
      So poets in the dropped tracks
of other poets stand, entering the pains

of slayer
    and slain: both are statuary still,
      angel's wings salt-bright in flight
or else stiffened in that pose imposed by air.
    The poet sees his own live parchments
      draw such nightly luminescence,
the spirit of what he may write, if he will.

Life along the Khlongs

(Tour F. River and Canal Tour)

Our boat glides from Oriental Pier
    down the Chao Phraya River,
the four of us rattling in its varnished pod,
the toothless old captain smiling from his place
at the tiller, his grandson on the gunwales.
    Where the guide points we will not look.
We gaze at the floating islands, trails
that the water hyacinths make behind us,
    the rotting barges, the battered pails

    let down from decks into that green/brown
    glass for the day's all-purpose
water. Whole families dwell in the wheelhouses.
Women cook their rice in that water, they bathe
babies in it, brush their teeth with it. We snake
    through branches that are alleys,
    spy on children squatting at their meal.
Incredibly, as we pass an embankment,
    I glance up at a man, hands on rail,

    the peach halves of his rump jutting out
    over that stainless medium.
Would I live here? We round a deck, deck or porch,
the wife crouched barefoot in the water that slides
across the floorboards as the whole river rocks,
    her teen-age boys bathing in it,
    nude or nearly nude as the water swells.
There is filth; there are rich smells; but the people
    look at us and there are always smiles.

Bird Vendors at Wat Phra Si Maha That

The December sun
is as full of glints and small birds' wings of light
as the gilt Buddha inside this temple.
Haloed, magnetic, immeasurably serene,
both sit in the bezels of their rings
of worshippers, their facets flaring
with the fire of topazes. Our faces shine

with flecks of goldleaf;
the air hums with it. In the courtyard, a child
flowers with the legerdemain of birds;
the small hands that hold the feathered milkweed pods
of their bodies seem to lift with wings
of their own in the pathways of our
faces. Hundreds of other birds are the brides

of cages; free them
and gain merit. The air is churned to froth as shoals
of them swim skyward. The space around
us becomes a grove of thorns as some of them
bristle at us, aiming for a place
to perch. Others island in the streams
of pilgrim feet that pass them, making a home

in the nest-formed dust;
they will not fly; they're caught in a simple trap
of fingers and are offered for sale
to free again. Perhaps the souls snared in the bonds
of these birds' bodies are so in love
with their Lord that they turn, as I would
to their land, to a heart-shaped home in brown hands.

Phitsanulok, January 1982

The Ruins of Sukhotai

The buildings are as though charred
by an unrecorded fire.
It is age. In such southern
zones the sun walks with a rage

that scalds the heart and the heart's
skin and sharply darkens stone.
Even the land looks old, low
and jointless, smoothed by the hand

of some fierce now-peopleless god
who settled here years before
the long-lobed god whose body
we see on all sides with its odd

unfilled mask that never was face.
He is changeless; changeless because
he will live, lives because he dwells
in souls that through their hands give

him this yellow offering
to wear, repeatedly new.
I walk among the finials
of submerged cultures. My young

country has nothing so still,
nothing so remote, no such
stage as these halls that crumble
even as I touch the walls

they recoil inside, recoil
from the always present I stand
fixed in here, as they move back
further and further every year.

What Is Written in Mist

Much the same effect may be achieved
by many sheets of fine silk gauze laid
        one over the other.
What you will note at first is the rivery moiré
        pattern like hair of separate colours
crossing them cascading together on the same
pillow. But look again: mountains melt in the airs

they are floating in, each mountain behind
a pane of mist a little milkier
        than the one in front
of it. Ancient Chinese landscape artists portrayed
        this simply by watering their inks.
You think this is pure convention, until you scan
the Yangtze Gorge, its walls gowned in clouds, its banks

completely bound by them. From the shrine
on Mt Kurama, the mountains across
        the mist are islands
drowned in foam. They are as indistinct as a solo
        viola playing arpeggios,
the orchestra under it held down to a hum. The mist
reaches our bones, as thorny as a locust is.

You shiver. I want to warm your hand,
hold you, but the thinly muffled years
        only accentuate
our distance, and I draw back. For a moment,
        you must have felt, beneath the accustomed cold
that glazes our eyes, the mountainous throbbing
of strings. You must know that I am also chilled.

We Will Not See the Cave

One touch, one touch passed between me and the wife.
    It started from the boatman.
    He brushed dust from my back. He brushed me
    and I acknowledged it; when he showed
me, always without speaking, that the wife's back
was also streaked with dust, that I should brush her
because I was closer, I edged toward his half

of the circle, unwillingly raised my hand.
    A simple gesture, that smile
    spread from person to person. The priest
    now waves his hand at the mouth of the cave.
He holds no light, so we will not see the scenes
inside he is describing. He does have light,
but he dislikes the husband. At tea, he screened

this man, found he was strong but would not draw near.
    The wife, the boatman, the guide
    and I shrink from the feel of the cave
    and move together; I am closer
than I have been to anyone for years. The husband feels
he can brave the cave. He cannot. He has not passed
the test of contact, he has nothing to fear.

Pagan, Burman, December 1984

A Publicity Photograph

Butch. You are no poet, you are not
sweet Thomas Chatterton blacking out
limply at eighteen across his bed
in the chiaroscuro of his attic,
you are Butch, the neighbourhood bully, whose threat

'I'll beat you to a pulp' simply because
I was the neighbourhood sissy almost
came true, his thumbnail inside my cheek,
his teeth clamped on my earlobe so hard
it must have been passion. You, at least,

have an easy smile and easy eyes.
But look, you have the same wire-haired terrier hair,
the same brutal brows, the same bull neck.
And why are you wearing that black leather
jacket and that black T-shirt that from where

I am standing reads '...lgar...' or '...dgar...'
in white? You are threatening me. I touch
my ear, believing your strong white teeth
made the scar there, I touch other parts
of my body, believing your hands can reach

me from where you are sitting in that white
kitchen chair, intimately. Your words
are full of subjected women who moan
as they twist around you but I believe
I could teach your body to lie still on the floorboards

or the moss-softened rocks as I lower
myself in the attitude of a cross
upon you, the fluttering white wings
of my chest beating against your chest.
I want that first real surreptitious kiss.

Saturday Sacrifices at Daxinkali

The worshippers with animals to kill
line up on the left bank of the brook,
facing upstream; the worshippers with flowers and fruit
line up on the right bank, facing downstream.
Together, they make up two long tusks
of a swastika. I enter on a third,
slipping on the mud, *my God, what is this blood,*

blood and body fluids, blood everywhere.
The temple has opened up its veins.
Kali, 'of insatiable appetite', is arms,
many arms waving at us, 'More! More!'
She tramps and stares, drools butterfat and blood.
She consumes essences: incense, purulence,
the smell of fear. I push through the crowd, for just once

She will sniff the smell of hate, my heart,
my heart alone among the amorous,
hating Her, stabbing at Her, the Terrible One.
Cocks crow, kids bleat, as I brush through silks
toward Her grotto. She is veiled in blood
and all I can see is one red eye, alive
with grease, glimmering at me. It is a look of love.

Night in the Shalimar Gardens

        Forster was afraid of the moon.
Not afraid, but as he said in a letter
to his mother, 'I always bear her absence
        gladly'. The scent of turmeric grates
on some: a blend of camphor, musk, and leafmould,
its oleaginous yellow-orange moons
across the water. Forster could hear the 'lutes',

        tamburas, and he could smell
the curries, the strong accent of turmeric
dominant in their near-harmonies, but starlight
        was no lamp, and they were forced to grope
their way over the causeway to the pavilion.
One imagines what a stiff Byzantine frieze
they were as they edged hand-in-hand, step-by-step

        past the oleander trees.
Certain details are missing: how one young man,
'an angel or the other thing', pressed him, palm
        against palm, in the dark. The sweet trail
lingered all through the meal, Forster's half-cupped hand
a pomander to sip from, to ward off eyes,
as he wondered how the rest of the skin would feel.

Do Not Doubt the Sanctity of Cows

The mullah curses.
    Calmly the woman-eyed ones
   turn their profiles on him. Bicycles,
jitneys, horsecarts, trucks, and cars swarm in on them;
    they will not move. Bells cross horns;
    no one crosses horns with them.
Head by head their eye-lined looks survey the street.
    Their slender-ankled armour deflects
     the crowd; no one will upset

their flanky beauty.
    Less a herd than a score-legged
   hydra, imperturbably they ford
the town; not once do they graze traffic. As we sit
    curdling in the sun, blocked by goats,
    dogs, men blocked by them, we wish
them gone, blasphemous thought! We will soak our sulk
    away in gardens, drunk on heavenly cakes
     made from the cream of their milk.

In a Sari Shop

Always with our eyes locked,
the shopkeeper's assistant
pours rainbows at my feet:
lustrous and sheer,
they turn to wine mother
in the light.

'What colour is the lady's hair?'
'Black,' I say, *like yours*.
He shows me one, jade white,
with morning-glories
along the border,
a symbol of legs intertwined:
his hand swims its shadow
beneath the fish's own white fins.

I notice that his shirt is broken
(my teeth could do that),
and through the gape
I see blue-brown breast muscle
over his heart.

The shopkeeper pours me rum,
offers to show me
how the lady should drape the silk.
'No,' I say,
'let him model.'
Mad with colour, or mad with heat,
I buy sheet after sheet of it.

Money: magic.
More rupees change hands
and later, at my hotel,
the non-existent lady
wears the white one for me.
Inside the opulent cocoon
I see all of his skin.

The Structure of the Décoration des Nymphéas

The surface is not water. It does not forge
water. It does not shimmer, tremble or shudder
as water does. There are the monstrous black-purples
and indigo-purples of rotten wisteria
only a half-choked eye might be forced to utter

as it dabbles its wings too close to the flame,
and wide, trowel-shaped slashes of cinnamon red
that surely have no place on water unless fresh
embers of war are falling there or the shadows
of a vermilion lacquer bridge. Webs of lead,

meant to collect the jasper-green and jade-green
glass of lily pads, enriched instead with fused
enamel and lustre in strange salamander shades,
bristle – they cannot float – above the shattered
malachite facets of the pond. We are used

to such encrustings, as though the efflorescence
of liverworts on stone or the rosepetal scales
that flake from fish, in the gold and cloisonné
work of Byzantine book covers or the altar
front of St Mark's, sometimes on the wings and tails

of Mogul enamel geese and ducks; we least
expect mosaics or shell cameos on cloth.
And yet, beneath this deceptively amorphous
web – we scarcely call it 'paint' – lie the fossil
Gothic bones of those years and years of behemoth

cathedrals that Monet so laboriously
reconstructed there: the pillars, arches, vaults,
braces, purlins, ribs and buttresses. Moated
inside the nineteen panels of his last work,
one senses the lack of wind, of sun; the faults

of colour that will never abide dragonflies.
Then, among those violet-rinsed greens and blue-browns,
a substance flows. It sounds with the solemnity
of sculpture but pulses with trills; and the eye,
and what lives through the eye, flies in it and drowns.

The Beard-Bristle Test

Jesuit and drill-sergeant, this man died hard.
His brothers in God commissioned me to write
him a eulogy, which I did. Monument
of respect (I did respect him) salted through
with fool's-gold, it was sounded off in high wind
by a priest who spoke with small *asperges* of spit,
his cassock whipping his legs like a broken flag.
The dead man lay indoors, untouched by diction,
mourned in concert with descant from mind to mind.

He said, 'A poem should make a man's beard rise
when he reads it,' a purloined thought he made new.
His own face was a boy's; it sweated its wax
as I bent over him in the crowdless church
and read him the real poem, a poem raw
with truths that grown men could not bear. These were:
love (not always brotherly); fear of the death cells
that bloomed in his bowels; and anger; little
sympathy. For three days after his beard grew.

One of My Sister's Poems

People in it stare at her,
I have seen it, I will not deny it,
I have been with her when she passed into rooms
and have seen the wings of their eyes perch
on her presence as though a cloak were on fire
in the air. And, if her hand was on my arm,
I felt that fire waterfalling in a whir

beside me with the native
sheen of silk, enhanced perhaps by gilt,
as an especially fine sari is, the few
pieces of costume jewellery she wears
turned to gold inside her Midas radiance.
At that moment I felt her grace rinse through me.
I was a matador about to dispense

a tricky and intricate
véronica. Robed with her eerie cape,
I stun everyone. And yet, in her poem,
she hides behind the ivory lace
mantilla of her house. Her neighbours see her pause
at the door, approach the yard; they do not know her
from poems. In Ecuador's rain forests, haze

hides rare orchids from man's gaze;
there are primroses rivalling gems
that hang in clefts so thin bees cannot get them.
My sister's poem survives the smudge
of my fingers, marks that show how my hands rove
over paper, feeling for the way she lives.
Someday I may decide those blurs mean love.

If Matisse Had Been a Dancer ...

He was a dancer.
Picture how he plunged his arms
in light as he opened his window
on the sea, the south. Colour.
Colour is the exercise of paintings, their feasts.
Yellow against violet, orange against blue,
contrasts exploded where small sunbursts

raked through the shutters,
through fan-shaped glass. After the long
Paris winters, he was galvanized
by the force of Nice. No water
was ever that pure tube blue. Arabesques
caper across the wall; the carpet two-steps
with the chair. Footlights cut through the dusks

of that old hotel.
Everything was fake, absurd,
delicious. A walk along the flags
was for his eye its notebooks.
From the first day there, he jotted down their red.
Back home among the northern greys, his new hues
lived. The heart has its own neighbourhood.

Hildegard of Bingen and Her Man

The manuscript was a bolt of new white wool
    between dark grey wool and brown,
   her robes and his, as Hildegard spoke,
   as Volmar made Latin what she said
and set it down. The manly letters emerged
    from stone, so sharp and so clear
were they, though Volmar pricked them with thorn and thread.

There was nothing flossy about her words. She dared
    admonish the Pope for church
   reform. Volmar trembled as the harsh syllables bled
   from his hand. With his white features bent
on holy embroidery, he might have been a girl
    preparing wedding linens;
Hildegard recalled her elder sisters sent

from home with hampers full of their handiwork.
    Yet, she had seen Volmar's arms,
   lightly muscled, furred with flocculent
   silk, and thought of her brothers with fight
in their eyes, wrestling. What she did not think of
    was his wifeless body, smooth
as hers beneath robes and as anguishing at night.

Watching Tintoretto's Bacchus Discover Ariadne

Suddenly, in the gold and marble excess
    of the Doge's Palace, three figures
arranged in such a way that their outstretched arms
form a triskelion, the delicate balance
      between flesh tone and sea green
    almost overwhelmed by candywork,
the appearance of a young man in a black
tank-top, light tipping the gold down on his biceps,
may distract the viewer. And, if his physique

is particularly faithful to the god's,
    whose kilt of grape leaves threatens to slip
from around his hips, if the faint scent of sweat,
rich but not rank, comes from the young man's body,
      seemingly magically to seep
    from the muscles of the god himself
the viewer may turn from the painting to look
at the young man, at first only because his presence
lends life to one of the figures, and he may speak.

Looking for Ezra Pound's Grave

      The dark exclamation points
rising above the water are cypress trees.
      Böcklin would have loved this scene.
He would have painted the trees as though their boughs
      were bear fur or half-dead galaxies;
he would have painted the church a just-baked brown
      against those fir-green sleeves. A sea breeze

      would bear the funeral boat
from the city, the cloaked figure in the nave
      heavy as a flag. I note
only the coloured photographs behind glass
      on the heads of crosses, the upturned graves,
exactly as though mass resurrection took place
      here, of those who cannot afford a space

      in perpetuo. This spoils
the reverent mood. The dahlias I brought seem loud
      now, though they are purple. I tramp
all through the Protestants but still I cannot find
      Pound's grave. I realize I do not care
and drop my flowers at a blank stone. I wonder
      who pays to keep his body in the ground.

Letter to an Unknown Niece

– to Pamela

Among the Manchu
 the mother's brother enjoys
  an especial place
of esteem; he is the protector
of his nephews and nieces, who chase

 about him singing
  songs to cajole and cajole
   him. Circling, circling,
they cry, 'Nuncle, nuncle, love me love,
small fried bread, seven, small fried dumpling

 give me, give me some!'
  So my mother's brother was,
   hanging just above
me cattycorner on the family
tree, bright autumn goldleaf (love me love!)

 among the green, more
  to me than my father, green,
   an elder brother
among the green, the rest of them green.
And I would love you like no other,

 sitting back in ash
  with you when all the green-gowned ones
   are part of the ball.
I would send you to your mousy task,
make thickly gilded traffic of all

 your yard's vegetables,
  but would keep you to myself, trying
   folk tale's smallest foot,
one foot slip slip in and slip slip out
a slipper of miniver as you put

58

the other on the fender.
    You would tilt up with your smiles my face,
        wanting to see there
on manhood's rock the imprint of ancient
fossil fern that is the face you wear

        from your mother. Gifts,
    many I would give; not long-sleeved fancies
        meant to catch love notes
from a prince, but real things, curious things,
from cornerless lands: ivory wind-boats

        that sink in water,
    Mandarin's robes embroidered with bats
        (they convey 'long life'),
a seahorse carved of jade, each wrapped
in illegible newspaper. No wife

        has received such things.
    They're the amulets a small girl dreams of,
        odd gems the potter
will not sell, bells the bellwright keeps, what the uncle brings
back from his alien life for his sister's daughter.

The Fight Between the Jaguar and the Anteater

    The Bororo call the Milky Way
'Ashes of Stars', and so it is, a hazy veil
    of dust clouds, curds, and congealing gas
10,000 light-years thick that waistbands the sky.
Between Scorpius and Lupus there is a bay

    of negative space that may be soot
strewn through the still-glowing ashes; it resolves
    into two animals, the jaguar
and the anteater. Shortly before sunset
the toothed one is on top, as though to assault

    the other, who is flat on his back,
but the relative positions are reversed
    during the night and the toothless one
is the master by dawn. An Iranxé myth
opposes two men: one represents the earth

    and becomes anteater; the other climbs
the World Tree to pluck the fruit that is the stars,
    he is shaman, he meets the vulture,
'master of tobacco', and becomes that stinking bird.
Toothless one, you walk around with your regard

    on the ground; you can never rise, as smoke
rises, for poetry is poison to you, the world's
    worst tobacco, it makes you faint. You can not
sit tree-high, vulture-winged, jaguar-glorious,
your mouth filled with keenness, smoking the universe.

One Middle-Aged Woman Opening Christmas Gifts

There is a Christmas tree in the lobby.
　　We agree to go down for tea
　　so you can open your gifts.
　Everywhere we go, ghosts go with us.
The people our ghosts were never would have guessed
we would one year spend Christmas in Korea.
You asked for nothing. There was one thing on your list:

　　forgetfulness. I cannot give you that.
　　We attempt to recreate
　　the feel of home, revive our ghosts
　and people the empty coffee-shop chairs.
It does not work. Festivity is hard to win.
Together with the warmth of reminiscence
come the bad times, regrets, Christmasses alone,

　　memories of Father and Mother angry
　　on Christmas day, Sister glum
　　or angry up until the end,
　my last Christmas with her. Mourning rules
the mood. I usually forget in different lands.
'Just one more beer' is not my life at tea time,
but I drink with you. We have always been friends.

In Songsan Crater

Wild horses are grazing in that bowl.
Lured by the thought that horses now feast
    where old fire fed, we push past barbed wire,
past signs that mean Keep Out, down into the core.
What looked from afar like plush is here waist-high,
    still silky. One chestnut stallion stands,
head down, a furlong from us. As we draw near,

    we see his coat glowing, ember-clear.
The same appeal that fruitwood's sheen
    has for us to touch, or half-banked coals
have for us to warm ourselves, now pulls at us.
My sister is first to give in to the power;
    the horse's flanks draw in her hands like gloves.
She did not know whether that sure sign of peace,

    hands out, palms up, would comfort the horse
or whether he would bolt. The same look
    that crosses the person's face, that marks
the horse, as the person reaches for the horse, passes here
between us, my sister and me, so many years
    have we been apart. She would welcome
my comfort or turn and run. I am still not sure.

Eve

Romanesque art (early 12th Century): Musée Rollin, Autun

Only in stone could this let-down matron
languish the way she does. From knee to elbow
she is as sturdy as a Roman aqueduct;
given that span from armpit to patella,
only the breasts, strapped on the way the breastplate
of a Wagnerian Valkyrie is strapped on,
      but tugged sideways, as though the faked

bulk beneath the skinny guest soprano's
armour were slipping, would tell you this is a woman.
Her face reveals nothing. Her mouth, kissed apart
by time or vandals, has dissolved into a small
sour moue; her eye, opening its shell to gulp
something, might be lewd, greedy, knowledgeable.
      It is her body, inert

but eloquent, that we listen to;
draped on the shrubbery of a petrified
manuscript, its shape reminds us of the twined
capitals at the chapter's head. Somewhere near
the fanged gut must be slinking, issuing his craft
into her ear, for urgently, but almost by chance,
      one pomegranate joins her hand.

Watching the Wayang Kulit from the Wrong Side

As *gamelan* music falls in large, soft drops,
its gathering torrent bubbling and gurgling
   across golden ingots and wooden bars,
the *dalang* slaps the lacy leather cut-outs
against the taut white sheet, and from the other side
   the women and the girls see shadows,
ruby and topaz shadows, a stained-glass crowd

like a windowful of Rheims Cathedral saints
snipped from place and set in motion by witchcraft.
   The women and the girls hear the same thing
we hear, the *gamelan* music swirling down
through its stony channel, unless xylophones
   and gongs appear to their ears reversed,
the surface golds drowned by the heavier browns,

and yes, they see the same thing we see, but dark,
turned round, they do not see the gilt glimmering
   from the figures in backlight as they twist.
Player after player pauses; smokes, chats, dreams.
The women and the girls do not see the men
   rising and passing, they do not know
what those faint shadows behind the shadows mean.

The Undertaker of Trunyan

His brown arm rests on my knee,
the skin smooth and buttery. As the boat rocks,
   alternately revealing field green
and green-over-purple mountain with its cowl
   of clouds cleanly cut off at the brow,
a pack of arms, like a many-armed Yama,
   stretches greedily across the prow

   for 'Money!' They say their dead
do not stink. There is cautery in the air.
   The undertaker leads me by the hand
to the body of a girl who died last night.
   It is true, their dead do not stink: a whiff
of musk, vinegar, and spice – a complex bouquet –
   drifts up from a bamboo cage, the life

   still left in it bronzed with flies.
As though selling fruit or bread, the undertaker
   takes me aside and plunges his breath
ear-deep for more money. These are clove trees, he says;
   they mull the corpses. In their shade, his youth
pours powerfully on me, its aroma
   boldened from the bone against the work of death.

Evenings in Kashgar

Like a golden florin
with two heads facing right
but opposite,
the horsecart driver and I
are obverse and reverse
of each other.

The horse
exhales the scent of ferns
from the afternoon.
His harness
is peppercorned with small brass bells
that bubble in the *brut* summer air:
dry seedpods
sizzle with seeds;
Ethiopian singers
are shaking their rattles.

The driver's face
is purple-brown against purple sky.
His profile, Greek,
grins a sliver of white
as I muster up his language.

Life is slowing down:
twenty years ago, or ten,
I would have been in love.
Shirts moonflower
from the arch-shaped blacks
of candleless houses,
but the tambourine monotony
of harness bells
goes on and on and on.

I lean my back
against the driver's back.
I feel wing muscles tense
as he pulls on the reins.
I gaze up,
but the tester over the cart
blocks the all-covering sky.
The trees
have their fingertips in silver,
so there must be a moon.

A Giant Is Eating the Moon

From time to time, the ancient Chinese said,
  the Dragon of Spring would bite the moon,
sometimes take it up by the mouth and gnaw on it.
The Chinese were a canny people: they could plot
the itineraries of stars, even predict
with accuracy the return of random
    planets; yet, when the dragon's jaws locked

around the moon, the clashes of pans
  rose from all the kingdom's sculleries,
and from the temples the barking of bronze drums,
to startle the dragon and force him to spit
it out. The moon was his to play with. A 'fire bead'
or 'fire orb', the size of a hen's egg, of course
    he would test its roundness between the lid

of his mouth and his tongue, never meant
  to swallow it. Still we do not think
the moon is a melon carved of flute-thin jade,
full of noctilucent liquor. A slice of it,
scooped of all its seeds, might easily explain
those juicy crescents that sailboat twice a month
    across the night. The clamour of tin

would welcome an occasional feast,
  as our faces peer skyward, countless
small moons stuck to earth. We leave too much to chance.
One day the giant who lives behind the sky
will dream of eating an orange and his hand
will finally appear and pluck the moon, dropping
    all around us bits of bright gold rind.

Overnight at Parangtritis Beach

The moon, borrowing its lustre from a source
    we sense with our skin but do not see,
    feels down along the shafts of rain clouds
        into the sea; the water,
bothered into leaflessness by the moon's plan,
    tosses the way the coconut palms toss
        as they shake off diamond.
    Your body skims with it. Like the shards
a boy skips across the taut sheet of a pond,

my glances skip by lensfuls over your bronze,
    stirring the underlife into bloom;
    hauled from your watery hold, you firework
        out in eerie patinas
on exposure to air. *Mare imbrium*,
    the moon's Madagascar, strays its dust
        into the fitful patterns
of a Han Dynasty mirror. The clouds
condense around our thoughts and clash. The beach burns

with the last of the moon and effervescence
    eats at us with terrible maleness.
    Windstruck, we run for shelter. Rain's weeds
        hang from us. We press so close
in the dark that your nerve ends permeate my flesh
    with their mycelia. I will swarm
        soon with your newest feeling
    as you revolve with me, my dark side,
refracting the night around us with your song.

The Sunflower

All summer you have stared at the sun.
Telescope with crêpe paper eyelashes flamed
   around the edge, your sun-disc disguise
was not clever enough; I have seen the inquisitive eye
     look up, look up, magnified
with wonder. The beautiful one in her bath
    was never safe from your gaze.

Backyard Renoir, Polyphemus among flowers,
I could have told you by September you would be blind.
   It has been overcast for weeks; the sun
is stored in you. The glowworms that work your roots
    are sparks again. Your face browns
beyond recognition, result of your madness,
    but your hackles still sunshine.

Your eye, heavy with accomplishments,
looks down, looks down. The memory stored in your crown
   is a fine essential oil that glides
clockwork toward perfection. Yet you are ruin.
    Your widower's weeds hang rags
from your hands. As though brooding on one great leap,
    you gather in and shed clouds.

At Gawdawpalin Temple

The boy flicks his flashlight at my feet;
even its sick, spasmodic glimmers bruise my skin
as the boy worms me up through slippery stairwells.
On the first tier, a family gathers to stare,
    to talk to me; they smile, tense, and group
for a photograph. One young man thumps his chest,
'Me, me alone!' and whittles brick with his heels.

He feels my eye through the camera cling
as his kilt clings; he strikes lightning with his pose.
These people ask for letters, but vows are what they want
when they bid me to remember them and bow farewell.
    The boy takes me to the top and falls
silent, as though he knew the accumulated calm
of centuries would leave on me its imprint.

A hint of what ails me has reached his mind;
what he has heard is the beating of an ancient soul
inside my bones. Down there inside the steep brown
shadows, I was old; my gracelessness on the stairs
    was proof of that. I look out where
my guide's eyes point and the vision holds my breath
so hard I cannot hurt. This moment is mine.